C000043103

PRAYER

GROUP STUDIES

LEADER'S GUIDE

Edited by
ANDREW ROBERTS

The Bible Reading Fellowship
15 The Chambers, Vineyard
Abingdon OX14 3FE
brf.org.uk

The Bible Reading Fellowship (BRF) is a Registered Charity (233280)

ISBN 978 0 85746 849 9
First published 2019
10 9 8 7 6 5 4 3 2 1 0
All rights reserved

Text © individual authors 2019
This edition © The Bible Reading Fellowship 2019
Original design by morsebrowndesign.co.uk & penguinboy.net

The authors assert the moral right to be identified as the authors of this work

Acknowledgements

Scripture quotations marked NIV are taken from The Holy Bible, New International Version (Anglicised edition) copyright © 1979, 1984, 2011 by Biblica. Used by permission of Hodder & Stoughton Publishers, a Hachette UK company. All rights reserved. 'NIV' is a registered trademark of Biblica. UK trademark number 1448790.

Scripture quotations marked NRSV are taken from The New Revised Standard Version of the Bible, Anglicised edition, copyright © 1989, 1995 by the Division of Christian Education of the National Council of the Churches of Christ in the United States of America. Used by permission. All rights reserved.

Every effort has been made to trace and contact copyright owners for material used in this resource. We apologise for any inadvertent omissions or errors, and would ask those concerned to contact us so that full acknowledgement can be made in the future.

A catalogue record for this book is available from the British Library

Printed and bound in the UK by Zenith Media NP4 0DQ

Contents

5   About the writers

6   Introduction

8   Session outline

| Lyndall Bywater

11   Week 1
An emotional outpouring

17   Week 2
The Solomon process

| Michael Mitton

23   Week 3
Raw and raging prayer

29   Week 4
Praying when we get it wrong

| Ian Adams

35   Week 5
Houses of prayer

41   Week 6
Change the world

| Carmel Thomason

47   Week 7
Focus on God

53   Week 8
Shining testimony

58   For your notes

59   Prayers

61   Creative media ideas

About the writers

Lyndall Bywater is a freelance speaker and writer, specialising in the subject of prayer. Having worked for ten years as The Salvation Army's UK prayer coordinator, she is now part of Connecting the Isles and works with the Europe team of 24-7 Prayer. She also heads up Canterbury Boiler Room, an interdenominational prayer community, and contributes to BRF's *Day by Day with God* Bible reading notes.

Michael Mitton is an ordained Anglican minister, a writer, a speaker and a spiritual director. He is the author of *Seasoned by Seasons* (BRF, 2017) and *Restoring the Woven Cord* (BRF, 2019) and is a regular contributor to BRF's *New Daylight* Bible reading notes.

Ian Adams is a poet, writer, photographer and Anglican priest, with a particular interest in nurturing practices of prayer. He is co-chaplain at Ridley Hall in Cambridge, Mission Spirituality Adviser to Church Mission Society and partner in the Beloved Life Project. He loves contemporary jazz.

Carmel Thomason is an author, journalist and speaker based in Manchester, UK. She has written *Anxious Times*, *Believe in Miracles* and *Against the Odds* for BRF. Other books include *Every Moment Counts* and the *Faith Stories* series with Archbishop John Sentamu for DLT.

Introduction

Introduction

> They devoted themselves to the apostles' teaching and fellowship, to the breaking of bread and the prayers. Awe came upon everyone, because many wonders and signs were being done by the apostles. All who believed were together and had all things in common; they would sell their possessions and goods and distribute the proceeds to all, as any had need. Day by day, as they spent much time together in the temple, they broke bread at home and ate their food with glad and generous hearts, praising God and having the goodwill of all the people. And day by day the Lord added to their number those who were being saved. **ACTS 2:42–47 (NRSV)**

Holy Habits is a way of life to be lived by disciples of Jesus individually and collectively. As Alison Morgan points out in the subtitle of her book *Following Jesus*, the plural of disciple is church. When Jesus calls us to follow, he gifts us others to journey with us, just as he gifted his first disciples – others who will help to teach us and who will learn from us; others who will pray with us and check how we are; others who will watch over us in love and keep us accountable in our discipleship. In the light of this, these Group Studies and the complementary daily Bible Reflecttions have been written for both group and personal usage.In this booklet, you will find material to help you as a church or a small group reflect together on the particular holy habit being explored.

The authors (who also wrote the complementary Holy Habits Bible Reflections; see page 62) have formed questions for reflection and discussion. Each author has selected two of the readings from the ten they wrote about and provided six questions on each for discussion. Some have a more personal focus, while others relate more to the church or group as whole. With questions of a more personal nature, you may wish to invite people to discuss these in the confidence of pairs and then make time for anyone to share a response with the whole group if they would like to. This

approach can also be a good way of making sure everyone has a chance to share if your group has newcomers or people who are shy or dominant.

You will then find a series of take-home questions about the habit. These have been collated from questions submitted by the authors, which mean they vary in style, tone and focus. As such, you may find some more helpful than others, so feel free to add or amend questions. As you work together, you might like to see what emerges in the responses and see if some of the questions should be revisited regularly (perhaps annually or every six months) as a way of reviewing the life of your small group or church as a discipleship community against the picture Luke offers us in Acts 2. Similarly, individuals could be invited to keep a journal to regularly reflect on their living of the holy habits.

In Acts 2:47, Luke says the believers enjoyed 'the goodwill of all the people', so there are also some creative ideas for ways in which your church or group could collectively practise the habit being explored in the local or wider community. These are thought-starter ideas, so be open to other ideas that emerge in your conversations.

You will also find some prayers and creative media ideas for this habit at the back of the book.

In all of this, keep your hearts and minds open to the Holy Spirit and be alert to the wonders of God's grace and the signs of God's love that emerge as, individually and collectively, you live this down-to-earth, holy way of life that Luke invites us to imitate.

Session outline

Session outline

One way your group time could be structured:

- **Opening prayer**
  (for example, the Holy Habits prayer on page 59)

- **Music moment**
  (see 'Listen', page 62)

- **Bible reading**

- **Reflection**

- **Discussion questions**

- Time for stories, testimonies or questions/issues that arise from the discussion

- Prayer

- Ideas to do as a group
  Spend a few minutes to agree when this will be carried out or to come up with other ideas

- Take-home questions/creative media ideas

- Closing prayer

| Lyndall Bywater

Week 1

An emotional outpouring

Read 1 Samuel 1:10–17

In her deep anguish Hannah prayed to the Lord, weeping bitterly. And she made a vow, saying, 'Lord Almighty, if you will only look on your servant's misery and remember me, and not forget your servant but give her a son, then I will give him to the Lord for all the days of his life, and no razor will ever be used on his head.' As she kept on praying to the Lord, Eli observed her mouth. Hannah was praying in her heart, and her lips were moving but her voice was not heard. Eli thought she was drunk. (NIV)

Reflection

There's something rather refreshing about praying with people who aren't used to praying out loud. I am part of a prayer community where some of our visitors regularly include swear words in their prayers. It can be a little jarring, and we don't necessarily encourage it, but it does challenge me to be more honest and heartfelt when I speak to God.

Hannah's story is one of the Bible's most famous accounts of answered prayer. She eventually gave birth to the prophet Samuel, and the rest, as they say, is biblical history. But at this stage in the story, Hannah is still more familiar with unanswered prayer than answered prayer. She has been asking God to bless her with a child for years. If you've ever prayed that long and that hard for anything, you'll know how easy it is for prayer to become dry and routine. Frustration and disappointment harden our hearts, and we can begin to shut ourselves off from the work of God's Spirit. Perhaps one of the greatest miracles in Hannah's story is not that she was still praying for conception after all those years, but that she was still praying with all her emotions engaged. We don't know if she was swearing, but the way she was pouring out her heart to God was almost as inappropriate, in Eli's opinion.

> Is there room for emotion in your praying, or has it become a matter of dry words and familiar routines? Hannah's brand of praying may seem risky; it makes us vulnerable and it opens tender places within us, but only when we pour out our deepest feelings can we truly receive God's comfort.

Questions

1 Have you ever spent years praying for something without getting an answer? What were you praying for, and what did the process teach you?

2 How can we as churches help each other and the wider community to come to terms with the pain and disappointment they may feel when their prayers aren't answered as they'd like?

3 Do you tend to express your emotions to God when you pray? If not, what stops you? What would make it easier to 'pour out your heart'?

4 When we pray together, what could we do to help people express their feelings to God as well as their thoughts?

5 If a non-Christian friend asked you why you choose to worship a God who sometimes fails to answer your prayers, what would you say?

6 Could you set up a prayer station where people who use your church building (or your workplace) can stop for a few minutes to pray? You could include some creative activities.

Idea to do as a group

1 Gather a group to walk around your local community, praying as you go. Split into pairs and walk a pre-arranged route around your local area. As you walk, keep your eyes and ears open to notice the things God wants to draw your attention to. As you notice the people and places you pass, pray for them, either in your own mind or out loud so your walking partner can hear.

When you get back to base, gather the whole group and share your reflections on the walk: what did you pray for and what did you each sense God saying to you?

Take-home question

1

When was the last time you found prayer easy and enjoyable? Think about where you were and what you were praying about. Why do you think that time was so special? Similarly, think about the last time you found prayer hard. What were the circumstances, and why do you think it was difficult?

| Lyndall Bywater

Week 2

The Solomon process

Read 1 Kings 3:10–15 (abridged)

At Gibeon the Lord appeared to Solomon during the night in a dream, and God said, 'Ask for whatever you want me to give you.' Solomon answered... 'Now, Lord my God, you have made your servant king in place of my father David. But I am only a little child and do not know how to carry out my duties... So give your servant a discerning heart to govern your people and to distinguish between right and wrong. For who is able to govern this great people of yours?' The Lord was pleased that Solomon had asked for this.   (NIV)

Reflection

The ancient art of storytelling often involved the hero being granted three wishes. It was a great way of building suspense, but it was also meant for the moral improvement of the listener too. You were supposed to share the hero's dilemma, work out which wishes you'd make in his or her place and so get a little wiser in the process.

Prayer is no fairy story, and we're certainly not limited to three wishes, but there is much to be said for thinking carefully about what we're asking for. God gives Solomon carte blanche to ask for absolutely anything: he can have riches to consolidate the wealth of his kingdom, victories to despatch any lurking enemies or popularity to shore up his reputation for generations to come. But Solomon thinks carefully, then asks for only one thing – wisdom.

Let's examine his process of reflection. First, he's realistic about his own limitations. Then he considers the calling God has entrusted to him. When he knows who he is and what he is called to, he can work out what he will most need, if he's to fulfil his God-given task.

When we're facing a daunting task, either as individuals or as churches, it's easy to make our prayers a shopping list of all the things we think we might need. Yet it can be helpful to use Solomon's process to refine our praying. Who are we? What are our limitations? What is the task we're called to? Which aspects of that task seem impossible?

> Take some time to answer those questions, and you'll soon know exactly what you need to ask God for first.

Questions

1 Who are you? Write down ten words or phrases which describe you: five which describe your strengths and five which describe your weaknesses.

2 What are your limitations? Write down the things which seem to be restricting you at the moment.

3 What has God called you to be and do at home, at church and in the wider world?

4 When you think about that calling, which part of it seems most difficult?

5 Having considered yourself and your calling, what do you most need God to give you or do for you, so that you can complete the task he's given you?

6 Write a simple 'Solomon prayer', outlining the thing you most want to ask God for, and pray it regularly over the coming weeks.

• • •

Idea to do as a group

1 Make a 'prayer box' – a box with a slot in it, similar to a postbox – and leave it in a place which is accessible to the public. (You could ask a local shop or café, or keep it in the foyer of your church building, if it's open during the week.) Put a pen and some slips of paper next to the box, and put a sign on it inviting people to write about people or situations they'd like the church to pray for and then to put the slip in the box.

Arrange to empty the box every few days and to pass the requests to a group of people who will commit to praying through them. (Ensure you comply with data protection guidelines, for example by asking people to anonymise prayer requests.)

Take-home questions

1

If God is omnipotent and sovereign, why do you think he wants or needs us to pray?

2

Is there a prayer you've been praying which hasn't been answered yet in the way you'd like it to be? What have you learnt about God through the process? How can we help each other to weather the disappointment of unanswered prayer?

| Michael Mitton

Week 3
Raw and raging prayer
Read Job 30:20–23, 26–27

I cry to you and you do not answer me; I stand, and you merely look at me. You have turned cruel to me; with the might of your hand you persecute me. You lift me up on the wind, you make me ride on it, and you toss me about in the roar of the storm. I know that you will bring me to death, and to the house appointed for all living... But when I looked for good, evil came; and when I waited for light, darkness came. My inward parts are in turmoil, and are never still; days of affliction come to meet me. (NRSV)

Reflection

Formal prayers in church often come over as technically correct and tick all the right theological boxes. While there may be a time for putting careful thought into our prayers, there are other times when our feelings are so strong that such prayers feel inauthentic. Some, maybe many, people, when they find themselves in the flood of such feelings, keep their mouths shut in the presence of God for fear they will offend him.

Job, however, is someone who will have none of this. He finds himself plunged into the most horrendous state of personal suffering. Friends come along to try to comfort him. They offer the official lines of the time regarding the problem of good people suffering, but these are of no use to Job. In his despair, he cries out to God, and some of his prayers seem shocking, such as in this passage. The friends are horrified that Job should say such things to God.

Interestingly, when God finally speaks, he is more offended by the friends than he is by Job (see Job 42:7–8), and he calls Job 'my servant'. Among the many things we learn from Job's story is that God can take our rantings and railings. For Job, expressing his anger and grief so honestly in prayer paved the way to his seeing a whole new vision of God. In the end, he needed not answers but a fresh encounter with the living God. Prayer from the guts is often the pathway to such encounters.

> Spirit of God, turn my raw feelings into passionate prayers.

Questions

1 Have you had Job's experience of crying out to God but failing to get any sense of God answering? If so, what did you feel about God?

2 Why do you think God sometimes seems not to answer our deep longings and prayers? What might be happening?

3 How do you pray when your feelings are strong (e.g. love, joy, anger, hurt, etc.)?

4 When do you find it hard to pray?

5 How have you found God has helped you when life has been difficult?

6 What is the emotional content of your prayers in church? Would you like these prayers to connect more deeply with our feelings? If so, how could that happen?

• • •

Idea to do as a group

1 Go out for a listening prayer walk – walk together or individually, but in silence, and see what God brings to your attention. What do you notice that you have not seen before? What is God saying to you about your neighbourhood? Meet back together and share what you have heard, sensed or seen. What are the cries of the heart of this community? Can you write a psalm that expresses the hopes and fears of your community?

Take-home questions

1

When has prayer felt very alive to you? Why did it? Share experiences of what brings you alive in prayer.

2

Why do you think God sometimes calls us to persevere in prayer (e.g. Luke 18:1–8)?

| Michael Mitton

Week 4

Praying when we get it wrong

Read Jonah 2:2, 5–7

> ' I called to the Lord out of my distress, and he
> answered me; out of the belly of Sheol I cried,
> and you heard my voice... The waters closed in over
> me; the deep surrounded me; weeds were wrapped
> around my head at the roots of the mountains.
> I went down to the land whose bars closed upon
> me forever; yet you brought up my life from the
> Pit, O Lord my God. As my life was ebbing away,
> I remembered the Lord; and my prayer came to you,
> into your holy temple.'   (NRSV)

Reflection

If ever there was a Bible story to encourage those of us who get it wrong quite often, it is Jonah. Jonah is told to go and give a message of good news to a people whom he believes deserve bad news. So he does his best to escape from God – by sea – only to find himself thrown overboard and gobbled up by a fish.

He spends three long days in the belly of the fish, and here he comes to his senses and prays this prayer, which is both a cry of help and a statement of faith. He tells God the story of his demise and the fearful experience of drowning. And yet, here in the dank, reeking stomach of the fish, he proclaims, 'Yet you brought up my life from the Pit.' Although he is still in serious trouble, Jonah nonetheless testifies to his being rescued, and he knows his prayer is heard in the holy temple of God. As we know, the fish does eventually spew out Jonah, and he goes off and does his prophetic business in Nineveh. He remains a bit grumpy, yet God still uses him.

There are times when we feel we have mucked things up and failed the God we want to serve. Jonah reminds us that, even in such troubled waters, we can pray to our Father, and in such praying we may well sense the first signs of his rescue.

> Lord, when I have messed things up, grant me the faith of Jonah.

Questions

1 What do you like about the story of Jonah and the fish?

2 Jonah felt the people of Nineveh did not deserve God's blessing. Who are the people today who some might regard as not deserving of God's blessing? What do you feel about them? What might God's word be to them?

3 How do you feel when you get things wrong? What helps you to recover?

4 How do you think God feels about you when you get things wrong?

5 Who else in the Bible got it wrong but recovered? How did God restore them?

6 How can our churches be communities that help us even when we get things wrong?

• • •

Idea to do as a group

1 In Jeremiah 29:4–7, the prophet called the people to 'seek the welfare of the city'. How can you apply this to your city, town, village or neighbourhood? What could you do to bless your local community? How could you improve its welfare?

Take-home question

1

How do you
pray when you are
lost for words? For
example, are you helped
by silence, speaking in
tongues, music, art?
How could you grow
in wordless
prayer?

| Ian Adams

Week 5

Houses of prayer

Read Mark 11:15–18

Then they came to Jerusalem. And [Jesus] entered the temple and began to drive out those who were selling and those who were buying in the temple, and he overturned the tables of the money-changers and the seats of those who sold doves; and he would not allow anyone to carry anything through the temple. He was teaching and saying, 'Is it not written, "My house shall be called a house of prayer for all the nations"? But you have made it a den of robbers.' And when the chief priests and the scribes heard it, they kept looking for a way to kill him; for they were afraid of him, because the whole crowd was spellbound by his teaching. (NRSV)

Week 5

Reflection

There are some places that seem to be particularly prayerful and holy. You will almost certainly know such a place. It may be grand and popular. It may be humble and largely unknown. Somehow, through a potent mix of atmosphere, architecture and history, such prayed-in places seem to draw us deeper into the presence of God, who is always present to us. They invite us to pray. And we should keep on returning to them.

If they draw us in, these houses of prayer also encourage us not to remain in them but to move out, carrying prayer and action with us. For me, the restored Benedictine abbey on the island of Iona is one such place. I love to pray there when I visit. But even as I pray inside the house of prayer that is the abbey, I find myself drawn to pray in the wider house of prayer that is the island. And as I pray on the island's beaches, on the machair or on the hills, I am drawn to pray for the house of prayer that is the wider world.

Houses of prayer are not given to us merely as holy places removed from the world. Rather, they must be 'houses of prayer for all the nations', drawing us in to propel us out in prayer and action into God's world.

> Which 'house of prayer' is a particular gift to you? How might you make sure that this house continues to be part of your life? How could your own home be more of a 'house of prayer'?

Questions

1 What are the tables you would like to overturn?

2 What might this passage have to say about the importance of buildings in prayer?

3 How does Jesus use scripture here?

4 Why did the religious authorities feel so threatened by Jesus?

5 How might this passage be an encouragement to pray with people of other faiths?

6 What did Jesus do that left people 'spellbound' by his teaching?

• • •

Ideas to do as a group

1 Take a creative, prayerful look at your church building. What might you do to open it up and shape the space so that it becomes a 'house of prayer' for your wider community?

2 Create a time to openly discuss what you are angry about. Commit to prayer and action in response.

Take-home questions

1
How could
your home, office
or studio be a 'house
of prayer'? (Feel free
to think about other
appropriate
places.)

2
What might
be the place
for anger in our
prayers?

3
How might
prayer be
mission?

| Ian Adams

Week 6

Change the world

Read Luke 1:46–55

And Mary said, 'My soul magnifies the Lord, and my spirit rejoices in God my Saviour, for he has looked with favour on the lowliness of his servant. Surely, from now on all generations will call me blessed; for the Mighty One has done great things for me, and holy is his name. His mercy is for those who fear him from generation to generation. He has shown strength with his arm; he has scattered the proud in the thoughts of their hearts. He has brought down the powerful from their thrones, and lifted up the lowly; he has filled the hungry with good things, and sent the rich away empty. He has helped his servant Israel, in remembrance of his mercy, according to the promise he made to our ancestors, to Abraham and to his descendants forever.' (NRSV)

Week 6

Reflection

The Magnificat, Mary's song of joy, is a powerful prayer of praise. Its opening has become familiar to millions of Christians: 'My soul magnifies the Lord, and my spirit rejoices in God my Saviour...' You may have said or sung a version of it this week. May this remind us to be people who pray our praises – and who pray them with joy.

It is also a prayer that brings change to the one praying it, and in turn to the world. This powerful prayer speaks of the change that has come the way of the young woman, Mary. Her experience is, of course, unique. But the pattern of this prayer can be ours too. Like Mary, the changes that God brings to us will, if we allow them, bring change to the world around us. You and I have been blessed – now may the blessing that has come our way in God's grace be a gift to others.

Through this series of Bible studies, a recurring theme is the need for prayer and action to sustain and to shape each other. This prayer is a manifesto for action. As we pray for our world, what would happen if we allowed the Magnificat to be a guidebook?

> How might the Magnificat shape your prayer and action as you consider the issues that face us as a society at this time?

Questions

1 Which line in the Magnificat particularly catches your attention?

2 How might it be a gift (and, of course, a challenge can be a gift) to you?

3 What does the Magnificat reveal to us about Mary?

4 What does the Magnificat reveal about the nature of God?

5 What does the Magnificat reveal about God's priorities for the world?

6 Is there anything in the Magnificat that surprises you?

• • •

Ideas to do as a group

1 Find ways to live out the Magnificat in your community. Offer people the chance to speak or write a line about how they would like to see the world changed for the better.

2 Commit to learning a version of the Magnificat and using it regularly in your prayer times. Reflect together on how this might be changing you.

Take-home questions

1
How might you incorporate joyful praise into your prayer?

2
Imagine Mary singing or dancing this powerful prayer. How might your own prayer be expressed more physically?

3
How do you sense prayer may be changing you at this time?

| Carmel Thomason

Week 7

Focus on God

Read Philippians 4:4–9

Rejoice in the Lord always. I will say it again: rejoice! Let your gentleness be evident to all. The Lord is near. Do not be anxious about anything, but in every situation, by prayer and petition, with thanksgiving, present your requests to God. And the peace of God, which transcends all understanding, will guard your hearts and your minds in Christ Jesus. Finally, brothers and sisters, whatever is true, whatever is noble, whatever is right, whatever is pure, whatever is lovely, whatever is admirable – if anything is excellent or praiseworthy – think about such things. Whatever you have learned or received or heard from me, or seen in me – put it into practice. And the God of peace will be with you. (NIV)

Reflection

There's double rejoicing here from Paul. Depending on your circumstances, you may add a third cheer or look on quietly thinking, 'That's easy for you to say.'

On learning the context of this letter, we understand that Paul's situation wasn't all calm seas and sunny days. He wrote these words while imprisoned by the Romans, not knowing when or if he would be released. The threat of execution was very real. Knowing that, it is difficult to grasp how he can feel peace. It does, as he says, transcend all human understanding. But Paul doesn't simply leave us with an unfathomable reflection of joy; he adds guidance for those searching for similar comfort.

He recognises we'll feel anxious, but advises us not to 'be' anxious, which suggests a state in which we've let our troubles consume our whole being. When facing great blows, that's easy to do. Paul understands this and adds that, to worry less, we must consciously think of something else. He suggests focusing on anything good, however small we may feel that to be, and being thankful, acknowledging God's presence in every situation.

Paul reminds us of God's closeness. He suggests handing our worries to God in prayer, while thanking him for all his blessings. Reminding ourselves of these things gives us confidence in God's love and goodness, so that we may rest in his hope and maintain our peace when storms come.

> Lord, however dark life seems, your light is always shining. Focus my eyes on your goodness, warm me with rays of hope and hold me in your peace.

Questions

1 Do you spend more time thinking over and/or talking about your worries with others than you do sharing them with God in prayer?

2 Are there things in your life that once felt like a blessing but have since become routine?

3 Why do you think Paul encourages people to focus on whatever is true, noble, right, etc.?

4 In the group, pray about any situations that are troubling you while holding a smooth pebble. When you feel ready, lay down the pebble in a central place to signify you have handed over the situation to God.

5 Spend a day looking out for and recording any kindness you experience, witness, read or hear about. Use your lists to discuss ways you can be kinder and develop deeper appreciation of kindness shown to you.

6 Think of someone you know who is anxious. How might you pray for them? And what could you give to them in terms of time or a gift that would help to reduce their anxiety?

• • •

PRAYER | Carmel Thomason

Idea to do as a group

1 Organise a creative prayer day with your group where you focus on what is good in your community and what you would like to see more of. Use these ideas to inspire a prayerful art workshop. Decorate smooth pebbles using acrylic paint, and seal them with clear varnish. Create the art around a central word such as, love, peace, joy, patience, kindness, understanding, hope – whatever comes to you during prayer. At the end of the day, put the pebbles in a bowl at the back of your church with a note saying, 'Take what you need'.

Each group member can take a pebble to help focus their prayer that week and a second pebble to leave in the community for someone to find. Encourage people to create more pebbles and to recirculate those they have taken, returning them to the central bowl before taking another for a different focus.

Take-home questions

1

French philosopher and scientist Blaise Pascal (1623–62) once said, 'No God, no peace. Know God, know peace.' What do you think he meant by that? How can a habit of prayer promote both peace of mind and universal peace?

2

'Prayer does not change God, but it changes the person who prays.' In what ways do you think that this is true? Have you experienced this change?

| Carmel Thomason

Week 8

Shining testimony

Read Colossians 4:2–6

Devote yourselves to prayer, being watchful and thankful. And pray for us, too, that God may open a door for our message, so that we may proclaim the mystery of Christ, for which I am in chains. Pray that I may proclaim it clearly, as I should. Be wise in the way you act towards outsiders; make the most of every opportunity. Let your conversation be always full of grace, seasoned with salt, so that you may know how to answer everyone.   (NIV)

Reflection

To devote ourselves to anything involves commitment, and here we see Paul calling the early church to form a habit of prayer, of which gratitude is core. When writing this, Paul had been imprisoned for up to three years. To speak with such clarity and joy in these circumstances demonstrates great mental strength.

In times of trouble, we can learn much from Paul's life of prayer. What he learned thousands of years ago through prayer and contemplation, research in positive psychology is only now revealing. Active appreciation can increase both well-being and feelings of connectedness, encouraging people to participate more fully in society, often in giving something back for the good they've received.

There is a call to alertness in prayer, being attentive to our situation and to the Holy Spirit's direction on our heart. Embracing prayer as a way of life means being sensitive to need and immediately taking it to God in prayer, asking for guidance and strength in any action we take.

There is a wonderful sense of community in this passage. Just as Paul prays for the Colossians, he asks them to pray for him too. The word 'outsiders' is used to describe those who don't believe in the saving grace of Christ. In a show of unity, Paul advocates embracing these people with our best selves, treating everyone well. To season food with salt in Paul's time was to make it more interesting and enjoyable. There is no one-size-fits-all.

As Teresa of Ávila (1515–82) said: 'Christ has no body now on earth but yours. No hands but yours, no feet but yours. Yours are the hands by which he is to bless us now.'

> Lord, let your Spirit shine through me so that, by my actions, others may come to know your love.

Questions

1 What would a devoted prayer life look like to you? What practical steps could you take to get closer to this?

2 Does your prayer life ever suffer because you are too busy, even busy doing good deeds? What could you do to create regular time for prayer?

3 Are you creating quiet space in your prayer life to be alert to the Holy Spirit?

4 What is it that attracts you to Jesus' message? Why do you think this message can be distorted?

5 Imagine any new people you meet this week have no preconceptions about what it means to be a Christian. How will you demonstrate Jesus' message in your actions?

6 This week, practise viewing any 'outsiders' you meet through the eyes of love. If you become aware of any needs of that person, pray silently about it. At the end of the week, look back at your encounters. Did standing strong in love change your view or behaviour in any way?

• • •

Week 8

Idea to do as a group

1 Even if you meet weekly to pray, finding a suitable time for everyone can be difficult. Extending the support network via telephone provides additional recognition of being always held in prayer. One way to structure this is for everyone in the group to agree to share telephone numbers, indicating hours when it is okay for them to be contacted. If something comes up in the week for which a member of the group would like prayer, that person calls someone in the group. The person contacted then calls someone else in the group, letting them know who initiated the prayer request and who has already received the message (this is so the same person doesn't get called twice). The message continues until everyone in the group has received the prayer request. As the idea is personal connection through prayer, it is best if the message is given by speaking to a person directly – not leaving a voicemail message or sending an email or a text. If the person you call doesn't answer, call someone else in the group.

Telephone prayer support also allows people who are unable to leave their homes for group meetings to participate in the group prayer and to be a part of this wider support community.

Take-home question

1

As prayer becomes a habit we begin to see our own needs and desires clearly as well as becoming more aware of the needs of those around us. However, it can be easy to fall into the trap of offering these needs to God without asking if there is any part we can play. For example, if you are praying for a more peaceful world how might you ask God to support you in creating more harmony and peace in your home, church and workplace?

For tour notes

For your notes

Prayers

The Holy Habits prayer

Endurance produces character, and character produces hope,
and hope does not disappoint us...
Gracious and ever-loving God, we offer our lives to you.
Help us always to be open to your Spirit in our thoughts
and feelings and actions.
Support us as we seek to learn more about those habits of the
    Christian life
which, as we practise them, will form in us the character
    of Jesus
by establishing us in the way of faith, hope and love.
Amen

A prayer of intercession

Lord, in our weakness we come to you for strength,
In our sorrow we come to you for comfort,
In our joy we come to you to celebrate with us,
In our times of anxiety we come to you for succour,
In times of confusion and doubt we come to you for guidance
    and help,
So now we come to pray for ourselves and others.
In Jesus' name
Amen

Prayers

A prayer for peace

Lead us from death to life, from falsehood to truth.
Lead us from despair to hope, from fear to trust.
Lead us from hate to love, from war to peace.
Let peace fill our hearts, our world, our universe.
Amen

Creative media ideas

Watch

Bruce Almighty (12A, 2003, 1h41m)
A comedy in which the eponymous Bruce, who spends a lot of time complaining about God, is given almighty powers to teach him how difficult it is to run the world. In particular, he has to grapple with how to answer everybody's prayers.

- If you had God's powers, how would you answer prayer? Would you want to say yes to everybody?
- Can all of our prayers really be answered?
- How does Bruce's experience of being God change his understanding of prayer? What important questions does God ask of Bruce?
- Did this film challenge you in any way about your own prayer life?

Read

Pray as you go
A prayer website with a daily podcast of biblical material, prayer and music to reflect upon and engage with; particularly good for reflective people (**pray-as-you-go.org**).

Listen

'40' by U2
A powerful song of lament based on the psalm of the same number, which repeats the cry, 'How long?'

Whole-church resources

INTRODUCTORY GUIDE

HOLYHABITS

MISSIONAL DISCIPLESHIP RESOURCES FOR CHURCHES

BIBLICAL TEACHING

They devoted themselves to the apostles' teaching and to fellowship, to the breaking of bread and to prayer.

HOLYHABITS

MISSIONAL DISCIPLESHIP RESOURCES FOR CHURCHES

FELLOWSHIP

They devoted themselves to the apostles' teaching and fellowship, to the breaking of bread and to prayer.

HOLYHABITS

MISSIONAL DISCIPLESHIP RESOURCES FOR CHURCHES

BREAKING BREAD

They devoted themselves to the apostles' teaching and fellowship, to the breaking of bread and to prayer.

HOLYHABITS

MISSIONAL DISCIPLESHIP RESOURCES FOR CHURCHES

PRAYER

They devoted themselves to the apostles' teaching and to fellowship, to the breaking of bread and to prayer.

HOLYHABITS

MISSIONAL DISCIPLESHIP RESOURCES FOR CHURCHES

SHARING RESOURCES

All the believers were together and had everything in common.

HOLYHABITS

MISSIONAL DISCIPLESHIP RESOURCES FOR CHURCHES

SERVING

All the believers were together and had everything in common; they sold property and possessions to give to anyone who had need.

HOLYHABITS

MISSIONAL DISCIPLESHIP RESOURCES FOR CHURCHES

EATING TOGETHER

They broke bread in their homes and ate together with glad and sincere hearts, praising God and enjoying the favour of all the people.

HOLYHABITS

MISSIONAL DISCIPLESHIP RESOURCES FOR CHURCHES

GLADNESS AND GENEROSITY

They broke bread in their homes and ate together with glad and sincere hearts, praising God and enjoying the favour of all the people.

HOLYHABITS

MISSIONAL DISCIPLESHIP RESOURCES FOR CHURCHES

WORSHIP

They broke bread in their homes and ate together with glad and sincere hearts, praising God and enjoying the favour of all the people.

HOLYHABITS

MISSIONAL DISCIPLESHIP RESOURCES FOR CHURCHES

MAKING MORE DISCIPLES

And the Lord added to their number daily those who were being saved.

HOLYHABITS

MISSIONAL DISCIPLESHIP RESOURCES FOR CHURCHES

Individual copy £4.99

Holy Habits is an adventure in Christian discipleship. Inspired by Luke's model of church found in Acts 2:42–47, it identifies ten habits and encourages the development of a way of life formed by them. These resources are designed to help churches explore the habits creatively in a range of contexts and live them out in whole-life, intergenerational, missional discipleship.

MISSIONAL DISCIPLESHIP RESOURCES FOR CHURCHES

HOLY**HABITS**

Original design by morsebrowndesign.co.uk & penguinbc

Bible Reflections

Edited by Andrew Roberts
Individual copy £3.99

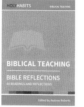    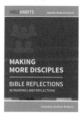

These new additions to the Holy Habits resources have been developed to help churches and individuals explore the Holy Habits through prayerful engagement with the Bible and live them out in whole-life, missional discipleship.

Each set of Bible reading notes contains eight weeks of devotional material. Four writers bring different perspectives on the habit in question through their reflections on passages drawn from across the Bible narrative.

Other Group Studies currently available:

Edited by Andrew Roberts
Individual copy £6.99

Group Studies and Bible Reflections for the remaining five habits
BREAKING BREAD | SHARING RESOURCES | SERVING | GLADNESS AND GENEROSITY | WORSHIP will be available in February 2020.

Find out more at holyhabits.org.uk
and brfonline.org.uk/collections/holy-habits
Download a leaflet for your church leadership at
brfonline.org.uk/holyhabitsdownload

Praise for the original Holy Habits resources

'Here are some varied and rich resources to help further deepen our discipleship of Christ, encouraging and enabling us to adopt the life-transforming habits that make for following Jesus.'

Revd Dr Martyn Atkins, Team Leader & Superintendent Minister, Methodist Central Hall, Westminster

'The Holy Habits resources will help you, your church, your fellowship group, to engage in a journey of discovery about what it really means to be a disciple today. I know you will be encouraged, challenged and inspired as you read and work your way through… There is lots to study together and pray about, and that can only be good as our churches today seek to bring about the kingdom of God.'

Revd Loraine Mellor, President of the Methodist Conference 2017/18

'The Holy Habits resources help weave the spiritual through everyday life. They're a great tool that just get better with use. They help us grow in our desire to follow Jesus as their concern is formation not simply information.'

Olive Fleming Drane and John Drane

'The Holy Habits resources are an insightful and comprehensive manual for living in the way of Jesus in the 21st century: an imaginative, faithful and practical gift for the church that will sustain and invigorate our life and mission in a demanding world. The Holy Habits resources are potentially transformational for a church.'

Revd Ian Adams, Mission Spirituality Adviser for Church Mission Society

'To understand the disciplines of the Christian life without practising them habitually is like owning a fine collection of soap but never having a wash. The team behind Holy Habits knows this, which is why they have produced these excellent and practical resources. Use them, and by God's grace you will grow in holiness.'

Paul Bayes, Bishop of Liverpool